River Light

poems

J. C. Olander

Poetic Matrix Press

Front Cover photo by J. C. Olander
Back Cover photo by Maureen Hurley

copyright © 2017 J. C. Olander

ISBN: 978-0-9981469-5-9

All rights reserved. No part of this book may be used or reproduced in any manner whatsoever without written permission, except in the case of quotes for personal use and brief quotations embedded in critical articles or reviews.

Poetic Matrix Press
www.poeticmatrix.com

Acknowledgments

I would like to thank the publications that have previously published the following poems: Shadows of Light, Jelm Press, 1985 ("What's the matter", "Mining the American"); One Dog Press, 1997 ("Salmon Fish 1957"); Poetry Now, 1997 ("Beyond Age"); Poetry Now, 2000 ("Between"); Kiss of Death Press, 2002 ("Camouflage"); NCPS-2003 ("Silver King Creek"); Rattlesnake Review, 2006 ("Parental Gift"); My Song is the Light, CPITS Anthology, 2007 ("Southwest Clouds"); Poems For All #757, 2007 ("Animal Grace"); Bird Words, CPITS Anthology, 2008 ("A Year of Haiku"); On The Other Side Of Tomorrow, CPITS Anthology, 2008 ("Toward Evening"); Lost Valentines, Six Foot Swells Press, 2008 ("River Dance", "Yuba Mother Gold"); Moving Thoughts, CPITS Anthology, 2010 ("River Dance"); Iris, Rattlesnake Press Chap Book, 2011 ("River Dance", "Visitation"); Trompete 8, Germany, 2014 ("Mining The American", "Stepping Out"); Thyrsus Press, 2014 (Broadside, "Silver King Creek"); The Word Boutique, 2015 (Broadside, "A Year of Haiku");

Many of the poems were recorded with or without music accompaniment on CD's. Spoken word: "Mass Man's Epiphanies", 1997; "Animal Tales", "Sierra Streams", "December Birds", 2013. Music accompaniment: "J.C. and the Apostles", various musicians, 2014; "Conference of Poets", musicians, Silent Motif soundscapes, anthology of six poets, 2015; "Highway to the Heart", musicians, Silent Motif soundscapes, 2017.

    I also wish to thank partners in poetry: Joyce Jenkins, Mark Baldridge, Will Staple, Bill Gainer, Kirk Lumpkin, blake more, Julie Valin, Maureen Hurley, Tina Areja-Pasquinzo, Eva Poole-Gilson, and all California Poets in the Schools for their individual support and inspiration all these years and to the many others who have supported me as well, too many to name here—Thank you All.

Introduction

Life is like a river—a river is like life—

The simple simile that means nothing and everything at once. Perhaps one of the oldest metaphors in human consciousness. What we put into a river's body is what we put into our bodies. Pure, clean water nourishes and heals our bodies physically, mentally, emotionally and spiritually; reflected light of our lives.

We could refer to water as a material commodity: an element, or an obstacle, to mine, use and make money as is rapidly happening with water privatization. Or, we could call it sacred—reverence its existence—regard it as beyond money's value or greed; that which allows us to live a good, healthy life, providing us with all of our necessities and pleasures; a sustainable balance: a miracle. We will have to choose which way to flow.

While hiking the central California Sierras from 1960's to 1990's, I never carried water with me. When thirsty, I drank from seeps, springs, streams, rivers where they flowed as I found them. In the 21st century, nearly all surface water is contaminated with harmful bacteria. When will we choose clean water for all species as a basic right for sharing equally and preserve as vital to our existence and well-being in the commons. Let the river flow with clear light.

Contents

Acknowledgments v
Introduction vii
Dedication xi

River Light

In the Beginning 3
Arden Ponds: Passage Rites 4
Salmon Fish 1957 7
Between 9
Sight Of Mrs. Breen 11
Ponderosa Grove... 16
Gilgamesh Logging Company—5 Millenniums ... 18
Raccoon Stew 21
Paul's Enlightenment 25
In Day's Grasp 27
West Escarp: Rockbound Pass Crystal Range 29
Blue Ripples 31
Elliptics 32
Parental Gift 33
Crystal Range... 35
Blue Fire 37
Silver King Creek: Upper and Lower Fish Valley ... 39
Two Fish Stories 41
What's the Matter 49
Tenaya Canyon 50
Michie Peak Myth 54
Graces in Yosemite 56
Blue Earth 59

The Vessel	60
Yosemite – Le Conte Lodge Ecology Poetics	61
Pilgrimage	68
Comets	73
Blue Breeze	75
Yuba Mother Gold	76
Visitation	77
River Dance	80
River Festival	81
Down By the Yuba	82
Camouflage	84
Stepping Out	85
Toward Evening	87
Native Cypress	89
Puzzled	90
Animal Grace	91
Each day our hands discover	93
River Light	94
Mining the American	97
Percival Creek	99
Sunrise to Arden: American River	101
Salmon State	107
Little stream	110

Author Biography

—for Jacquie

whose river dances with pure light

River Light

In the Beginning

Crystal serpents journey
    heaven's terrain—till
        ocean pounds its sudden depth

Electric bolts bubble
    the cauldron sacred spark:
        flesh thrust
cougar's urgent snarl
    carves Sierra scarps
        coursing scree scars—

A soft breeze illuminates
    the black oak leaves rustling
        scattering flames

Their branches nourish
    seasoned ideas:
        insects moonlight glows—
stars swirl through dark matter
    possibility sparking
        my brain rivers

Arden Ponds: Passage Rites

While riding my bike
on the American River's
bicycle blacktopped trail
from the old oak grove below Fair Oaks
up on the banks of sand
as it turns north down over gravel
around south across the bars
west rising, falling, turning
through tailings dredged for gold—
a rider approaches: an old wrinkled face
I remember in cottonwood leaves of August
in the Pacific Gravel Company's diggings
where I fished in swamps and ponds
with skunks, snakes, turtles and raccoons
a poised blue heron—bull frog
kicking, gigged on the point of my spear.

From the lodge of beavers I dove in a pond
and swam into willows—rose in the shadows
to a shower of light through branches and leaves—
"Gotcha!" – he jerked me by my arm
through branches over fallen limbs—
I bounced up the embankment
tripped over rocks, stumbling
through star thistle needles, poison oak
to his car—scared, gasping for breath
his bony gripped fist shook me
I peed my pants—I had trespassed.
He sneered in my eyes—I wept.

Then he let me go! Grinned and told me
"Now git! And don't come back."

So, I followed the road ruts
out of his sight—cut to the river
through brush and gullies and turned
upstream where it bends with rapids.
I dove in the ripples to wash me clean
restore courage and keep me cool
for the animal trails
through cottonwoods and willows to the oaks
where ivy nets and blackberry vines
weave a clearing—a stone's throw
to the gravel road he patrolled, billowing dust
in a '48' Chevy coupe, army-olive green.
I busted a window—yelled my coup
across the mud and cattail clumps
and a field of thistles
broken with gullies of nettles,
five o'clock sun silvering their fiery leaves.

He stopped—jumped out, scrambled up
on the patrol car's fender
dust cloud billowing, swirling around him
fists clenched, muscles, face taut—yelling.
I laughed at him—held high my stringer
of bigmouth bass, golden bellied cats.
He swore and cursed.
I vanished.

Now it's all gone.
I pedal my bike

on the American River's
bicycle blacktopped trail
through subdivision sprawls
and fresh green fields
control-burned each autumn
an orchard five years before
but the pears we picked
or was it plums?

Our eyes pass
vanish—

Salmon Fish 1957

Salmon rose waves up river
in Arden bend's green, deep rapids
their dark crystals shimmering
rite of passage—American River.
Silvery, red, ripe and huge
so good to eat—Salmon
in the fall's gold morning air.

Cool cobblestone bar
granite, quartz, serpentine
sand of schist mountains
mineral rivulets—willows
quivering river's flow.

A fin wake!
Narrows up dredged channel
splashes shallow turn
quickens toward current's pull—
wild in the emerald waves—
I splash in
plunge knife into its body
thrashing its shimmering scales
scarleting my arms and legs:
christening—American River
water and blood of our lives.

I pull its body
bleeding and exhausted
from the current's soft swirl

up cobblestone to sand.
50—60 pounds?
I could not hold it long
from the ground to my jaw
at 5'6" and 12 years of age.

A black and white priest
emerged from the willows
on the shore line's gray shaded stones
paused.
"What will you do with such a large fish?"
"Eat what I can carry home," I replied
and offered a share to him. He declined
not dressed for Communion's flesh.
He blessed us all as I cut thirds
ate a portion of Its Sacred Roe:
the River's Creatures eat It All.

Between

Dawn flares
ridge pines
splinter light
blue oak limbs
angled shadows
canyon granite
fractures
stream gravel
riffles between
cattail stalks
centered
in tangled
blackberry thicket
yellow-black orb
weaver spins light.

    *   *   *

In valley's
evening breeze
through garden café
black mesh
stockings
scissor aisle
April moonlight
gardenia bloom glow
Chablis glass—ting!

    *   *   *

Between cliff
and waves

gray pebbled beach
twilight cold
calling gulls
fly up
crab shells
picked clean
ebb-tide dissolves
light splinters
pine ridge
flares dawn!

Sight Of Mrs. Breen

*"Never take no cutoffs and hurry along as fast
as you can."* — V. Reed
*"Why? — Because they have no mountains of
their own."* — J. Montoya

I woke up in the twilight driving hard
up Donner Pass feeling pit bull bad
so I stopped and scrambled up a mountain—dawn light
breaking where I thought a vision could be had.
But when my climbing reached the top
wind was gusting screaming wild
lightning cracking split the sky
and granite snow began to fall—
I slipped into a rocky crevice fast
like a mountain marmot scurries
rolling eyes to catch a shelter niche
until this raging swirling snow
passed me by and I could go.

I can't say how long it raged
could be one or several days
when it cleared my sky was dark
I thought I might be in some hero's maze.
No star shining showing me the way
then I saw a body lying burning in the snow.
I thought it might be hell or heaven's torch
but a closer look it was a woman
and her lips were moving syrup soft
glowing with some fiery light
so I laid my body by her side—
well, to keep me warm if nothing else
maybe catch a little of her mystic tale.

I'm not sure how long I laid
could be one or several days
till I saw the waning moon rising fierce
howling for some kind of praise.
I tried to mouth a cliché slogan
why I'm lying by this woman's glowing body
in the snow up on this narrow cliff ledge
but the pines began to moan a ghastly rock tune.
Thunder rumbled in the mountain's heart
shaking hard to skid us down its black ice chasm
so I rose up to my knees—hands shaking high
crying I love living don't kill us please
I want to leave—where's your keys?

No sooner screamed and it was granted
sunlight's rising from a riffled river
freighten putrid sewage in its heavy water.
No, no, I didn't do it! I would never
ever pee or throw in glass, paper, plastic
metal, garbage, any litter in its water.
It didn't matter what I screamed or pleaded
'cause its splashing said I better clean it!
No, no, I'm too busy, wife and kids and job and computer
but the river grabbed me in its oily water
shoved me through a narrow canyon to a normal city
big or small, I didn't know where—I was everywhere.
I started choking, stumbling, mouthing metal air.

When I awoke, I had no wallet
but I had a heel print on my face
with a neon god in uniform grinning down strange.
I said, "I want a lawyer who can represent my case."
No sooner spoke, his knuckles started teaching me my sense.
Yea, I earned my degree, but I could not stand to walk

so I started crawling down a canyon gutter sniffing
for a bit of food to keep my strength.
I got lucky at a corner restaurant booth
a new age chef slipped me a slice of paradise
before I turned to scurry on my way
I smiled sly, twitched a wink of thanks.
He replied, "Your desires procreate insurance banks."

Me, I ran into the city center
sirens streaking canyons piercing glass
shattered fragments fell around me flashing
faces falling to the city slashing teeth mass
spitting grotesque colored flames off their tongues
in white, yellow, red, brown, black and blue
mixing in the city center cauldron
boiling steam like some giant's party brew.
A golden flute piped, "He's on his way home to supper
with gambling blues—Foreign's Wolf snapping at his heels."
I shinnied up the city center status spoon
praying, "Can you save me with a Francis Scott Key?"
the party's chorus brayed, "Tickets go for hawker's fee."

I never carry any money but I'd seen enough
to deal a trade so I smiled a little coy, said
"Hey party boss, I'll give you what you want
if you come on home and lie with me in my bed?"
He rose, replied, "I'm appalled, you crazy,
spreading disease?"
"Huh?" I said, "I've ridden every line from east to west
and back again but gliding home on steel
through the snow scene's the power rush for me."
His eyes got big as saucers and he licked his lips, smiled,

said, "I'll let you ride as baggage on my corporate train
if you can prove that what you say is true."
Well, I'm not good at telling tales
but reading eyes, I know when someone's seeing sales.

"It's a deal—but you better pack your nose with sugar stuff
cause we're rolling over bloody bodies stinking in the snow."
"I'd rather hustle quickies in martini bars," he said.
"No, no," I said, "You sold our word—now we gotta go."
Across sand rivers, concrete plains, skeletons glare hollow
eyes then a farmer in a covered wagon with his family freight
hollered, "Our farming soil is dead, we're moving west."
Party boss agreed, said, "Shed your blood
eating what you want!"
But at the mountain peaks, snow blocked the pass
I said, "Your words sing true as rock." Then I left him.
He's cutting trees and moving mountains
for his loco-motive train.
I wove on willow snowshoes headed for the pass
and the woman.
He called me, coward, a lazy queer and yelled,
"A man is a man."

But high up on a snow ledge, I found her frozen, glowing
body with her syrup soft lips whispering what I had to know.
She said, "In my soul—Wilderness!
In this heart of snow—
Slashing canyons in this rock
rippling emerald pools—

Drink my crystal's flame
from this sea's dark waves—

Sun, moon, stars, turning time—
Kiss my body's lips and feed our fire
before I have to leave—my name is Mrs. Breen!"
I said, "I will. I can speak your words well.
But what do they mean?"

Ponderosa Grove

Twenty columns
yellow-orange-brown-beige
150 plus years—new old growth?
First cut for Iron Horse's rails
500 year old trees—his-story!
Cinnamon rivulets mesh bark's
puzzling design structuring
transpiration: water into wind
through rich green bristle needles
sparkling deep blue pool's
oxygen—April clouds sprinkling
basalt spiked ridge:

   it's the water cycle boogie
      going round and round
   the water cycle boogie
      going up and down.

   Evaporation—transpiration
      condensation—precipitation
         saturation—round and round
   it's the water cycle boogie
      going up and down.

Orange, red, lime lichen abstracts
pattern ridge rock towers—match
patched manzanita intersperse
cirque sloped, red-purple talus
breaking down mineral grits

feeding young old growth grove—-
twenty ponderosas, all that's left—-
splendid specimens shinning
before the phallic blade:
arrrrrrrrghghurrrrrrrackkkkkkkkk——
Forgive us Father—our sins.
Our blade must fall!

Gilgamesh Logging Company—5 Millenniums

*Gilgamesh: hero of Sumerian epic—
first written in cuneiform 2600 to
3000 bc in the fertile crescent—
Assurbanipal, Assyrian King, 700 bc
is main source.*

Industry's smoke/smog chokes west coast
three months—near November, storm approaching
we flee up California into Oregon, 101.
Maples, alders, oaks golden metal sky
one mile inland, vanish up canyons in
clear cut quilt work.

Log trucks roll by, down shift, up grade.
Diesel over hauls our generations' harvest.
Saplings under fourteen inches—third cut
re-growth: chipped, mulched into toxic stews:
glued particle board construction for suburbs:
pollution—dilution—solution: toxic home
syndrome kills.

Steel skeletons slough corrugated scales:
logger relics rusting sawmill compounds
in vacant lots outskirts of town: superfund.
Up slope, robots track plantation products
take what's left: quick killing in Xmas trees
soak up holiday cheer's merriment: bonuses
south of the border down Mexico way.

Meanwhile, RV asphalt parking lot crumbles
into Winchester Bay—we're taking showers
on guard, checking out sights on tools
winning the race west extracting resources.

Acid clouds dissolving centuries obscure
forest for trees.

Into the green forest mist—Gilgamesh
entrepreneur, prince of Uruk Inc. with
side kick wild man, Enkidu, ten steps behind
hunt the heart of the woods: terrible Humbaba
keeper of the Sacred Forest Primeval.
Gilgamesh, proud and golden one
fourth in line from the great flood.
Son of Lugulbanda, sets his name
where no man's name is written:
scrawls his motherland's face
for fame, fortune of his own making.
Subdue an evil proclaimed to the land
where the way was broad, the going good
and the ancient ones grew strong, wise
revered through centuries.

Awed for weeks our two young heroes
wander amazed; then, cut the first tree.
It thundered to the heavens—shook
the mountain's core to its very spine.
Terrible Humbaba, keeper of the forest
let out a wail—slapped his thigh in scorn.
For he knew his time was done
Goddess and forest would fall.

For the fragrant gates of mighty Uruk
brought down by great Sargon—
Sacred cedar walls: Solomon's Holiest of Holies
Assyrian ravaged, burned to the ground—
Galleys of Persian hordes, the Greek raiders

sinking to the Mediterranean's blue abyss—
Marseilles' Sacred Groves falling
Caesar's blade spares nothing to his fate—
Cornering the market keeper's share
new world plunder in catacombs of our mines—
Civil obedient conformity rules as forests are raised.

Raccoon Stew

At Ski Run Blvd. and Pioneer Trail
spring morning's light glows
from Heavenly Valley—Tahoe's deep blue!
Saturday cartoons scramble
from my neighbor's apartment—
the three sisters, "All American Girls"
2, 6, and 8 years old, suck its milk—
the violence blackens their teeth smeared
red with TV breakfast: cherry cotton candy
cherry Popsicle and a Lucky's cherry pie.
Their father is a working man;
he sits on the sofa, sips suds
as the wife, worth fighting for
clears up last night's dishes.

Outside, over their heads, light shatters
through needles of three huge yellow pines
littering cones and needles across
sage cluttered sand-drift into pine shadows
beyond the asphalt Pioneer Trail.
"Daddy, raccoon," wails the youngest.
"You girls don't go out and play with it.
It'll bite-cha."

From my window, last night takes shape:
my neighbor, driving us home
from Fallen Leaf Lake—late fishing—
a clear starry night closed in on
"Coons!" His headlight beams caught

them jolting left across the line.
He guns his engine as the bright beams
chase one of four, "He's a big one,"
up a sapling cedar. "Coon stew,"
he barks—brakes the car. We leap
out the doors—I am stunned to watch.

My neighbor's 31 years lumber
into the light, mouth open, breathing hard
suspendered in plaid shirt, he stoops
gropes dark shadowed ground for a tool
rises, looking up, his new full set of dentures
gleam moon-like as he steadies his angles
in stiff brush up against young firs and cedars.
A large fractured rock fits his right hand.
"UUNNGGHHH," he throws it—sshhhhhiessshhht
thump! Shh-craaazzzzzcchhh—the coon falls to his
feet. "I got it! I got it! Coon stew!"

He lifts a larger rock—his two fists grip
slab-like, white broken granite glistening
in the head light—over his head
and thrusts it, "UUGGHHNNMMM—thum-uh!"
"Kerrraaaaaaahhhhhhh," gags the coon.
"Get that box out of the back!"
"Huh?" I am still struck stunned
triangled in the car's open door.
Again, the rock rises and falls, "Thum-hump!"
Cabin lights flash—glow icy in dark silent forest.
"Let's go," I whisper loud.
"I'll get it," he barks. "I got a coon stew.
I know he's dead. I bashed him on the head."

The drive home fixed the bag's image.
His aim was true but strange.
The body in the box thumped a bit in the trunk.
"We got coon stew, no fish, but coon stew, Haaa!"

Now, in spring's morning light
the coon leans hard right, hobble
stumbling towards a blur of May aspen trees
green-gold leaves flickering in cool breeze.
Fifty yards further on, the coon will be gone from here.

"Look daddy, blood's all over his head,"
yells the oldest sister. My neighbor's rough.
He grips an aluminum bat as he walks out
beneath the largest of the three pines
to poke it—it trip-falls—staggers up—leans
hard left—staggering forward-faster—falls.

He probes it and the coon gags—wheezes air
but rises, stiff legged, continues
circling back into the box as the sisters
circle it, jumping and shouting excitement.
But now, he can't kill it. The sisters
plead for its life and my neighbor has no
answer. I step outside and tell him
"I'll take it into the forest. It belongs there."

In the cool light of the aspen grove
the spring fed stream gurgles—the coon
stumbles from the box into the sandy shallow flow
and drinks long and slow. "What can I say?"
but touch it; tell it, "I'm sorry for your pain."
It hobble-stumbles into the grove's deep green grass vanished.

*   *   *

Two year later, on the job site at Harrah's Hotel erection
a bitter March wind sings in its steel skeleton
icing the 12th floor concrete snowmelt.
Its bare metal burns against my skin.
Here, I hang sheetrock to its galvanized frameworks.
My neighbor works as a machine operator:
backhoe and crane.

On that day, 4' x 12' sheets of rock
stacked like decks of cards on the 18th floor
blew off—fluttering over the edge like confetti
smashed on the asphalt parking lot. But,
it was the crane's ball and hook that did it—
at lunch break, as he walked across the fenced in
ground of the job site he knew so well—shattering
his helmet and skull when the cables let loose
the weight fell silent in the wind. But the iron screech
and the yelling, gathering crowd—did he hear that?

What caused it? No matter in that.
He lived, not remembering the impact.
Nor could his brain feel the steel plate
riveted to his skull encasing the gray matter.

After work, I returned to the grove and stream
where the coon drank and I knelt on the sand. I
looked into my reflection and drank long and slow
the sun's last rays melting the last snow on this Sacred
Ground, the aspens, naked in the cold spring's fired sky.

Paul's Enlightenment

Paul became enlightened last June on his holiday vacation
when he escaped from his eight to five work week
creating bureaucratic data-graphs concerning social controls.
He wanted to experience — "Who am I?"

He bought a ticket on one of the 75 daily collection buses
up to his favorite "Paradise Playground in the Sierras,"
lake where everyone feels refreshingly rejuvenated in
99.9% pure aquamarine, green, blue, purple hues.

He arrived in the fun, food, fortune center but rented
a bicycle and rode out beyond the sprawled flesh
across public beaches festering tourist inflammations
to a scenic beach away from the maddening crowd:
the natural, pristine, Hidden Beach, called "Nudie Beach"
by spectators who just happen to be in the area walking
the dog to relieve the animal's manuring imperative
and certain uniformed officers brandishing binoculars
congesting traffic at nearest public road views, no turn out,
two patrol cars, tires crushing vegetation,
eight hundred yards to the beach—
peering at the beach, quaking aspens, marsh
and bird sanctuary with scattered willow clumps between,
to spot naked browning bodies frolicking on the
golden sand beach splashing snow-capped crystal waves.

Paul began to enlighten the moment he removed his clothes
and dove into the 99.9% pure lake—muddied with human
swarms churning dirt into dust into mud, gouging out property

lots, installing faulty sewage designs, driving automobiles
dripping oil, spilling gas, spewing fumes, roaring motor boats
regurgitating iridescent gas-oil shimmering surface sheen,
disposing potato salad, fish entrails, cans, bottles, urine, soiled
plastic coated diapers, herbicides, insecticides, hooks, lines
and sinkers into its 99.9% pure, dark, cold depths—surfaced
flip-turned, walked out slowly—grainy sand tingling his soles
bubblegum wrapper clinging to right shoulder, slick, green
algae wrapped round right knee, pink shreds woven into its
fibers—sliced left instep on thin, clear, shattered glass point
of broken beer bottle, painlessly deep till water stung
and dark blood colored wet, golden sand scarlet.
He sat down beside a fresh dog feces squished
by the black boot sole of a certain uniformed officer
arriving on the shoreline to award Paul his citation
for enlightenment and extort a $500 promissory tithing
for pilgrimage privileges to atone for his deviant
rebirthing ritual.

Paul enlightened in noon heat, meditating, bleeding
on the golden sand shore of the Sierra's Paradise
Playground in the Sky Lake.

In Day's Grasp

At Pioneer Trail
   and Heavenly Valley
walk between two ancient Ponderosa
   gateway through sage brush
      scent smudged centuries
into spring brook's
   aspen grove
      few know in Tahoe.

Clear April morning
   breeze fluttering
      leaves quaking-glittering—
bony white limbs
   rattle—sunlight
      slivering emerald veil's
chimes—spears
   sapphire Steller's Jay
jeweled in cove crystal

Paused—
   to quench thirst
grounded—mesmerized
   in sand's sole massage—
beetles buzz
   the white trunk maze
      green long grasses singing
   arpeggios—millions
aspen flames
   applauding the sun

paused me too—
   brook bubbling
      musical obstacles
sticks, needles, turning
   crystal melody—
the wind's rush
   rippling pool—
      leaves submerged
in sunlight, trickling—

But one more step—
   hold its brilliant
      pulse in hand—
Snaps twig!
   Springs it to a log
      flutters to bush
bouncing along a flimsy branch
   flicks wings
      to reach a limb
pause—turn
   our eyes meet.

Too stunned to scold
   it shivers
      trims tufts
prolong what mock it can muster
   from the green veil doom—-
      flies through flickering leaves
   into sunlight—
air chills.

West Escarp: Rockbound Pass Crystal Range

January's
clear air
raws skin

ax-cut
foot
holds
down
steep
cirque
slope
snow
between
crag
ice
falls

chhhk—chhhk
chhhk—chhhk

pale orange
sky fades
dark
descends
void
rock-ice

forest
ridges
etched
Silver's
forks

great valley's fog
coast range peaks
and over all
Venus shines!

Blue Ripples

Blue ripples the green field
   wild horses gallop into clouds

the long winged geese lift
    over reeds and willows of the great valley's marsh
       destiny's magnetic symphony

and the stampeding mustangs
   beat their drums upon the prairie
      of the rolling rhythm of freedom—

Through aspen leaves dangling the sunlight's hordes
   caressing the landscape's resilient flesh

the Truckee River swift current
    Aprils canyon stark cliffs:
       snow melting from heart's isolation

a luxurious bluish-red
   stone river polished
      comforts a clenched fist.

Elliptics

I searched books
relic pages
saints fingered—
scoured leaves
scribes scribbled—
all in vain
I was not flamed!

Till sunset blazed
the eye's storm:
salsify opening
elliptical enlightening
encircling seeds—
the wind whispering
"I am the seer!"

Parental Gift

My two sons follow me along spring trail
through tall grass and willows to Cold Creek.
Two children balancing give and take
along this stream feeding Lake Tahoe.
They're learning to swim—I teach
and learn river languages and character
of watershed bodies exchanging energy.

Where it snakes slow in deep turn
widens—pools—then narrows power
to overwhelm our capabilities to recover
what we give into for our needs and desires
adapting to a chosen way of measuring
our intelligence in its clear, cold current
rushing into thicket danger.
Death is always present.

We work for what's desired—call it
Baptism in Mysterious Beauty:
what swirls grace lingering in a sand cove—
sculpts rock words—designs calligraphy—
tiger sense in lily—wood—image—our flesh.
We remove our clothes—enter Its Garden:
learn naked way of existence.

A son clutched to each palm
we wade in up to their necks—
swing and swirl them through stream's
thrill in cold spring water exciting skin

shouts breaking light through willows—
two twirling gyroscopes circumference
parental circle's center of being
in hand's grip of trust—current balance:
economics in watershed integrity—
diversity's health and welfare.

Hurl them up stream from my grasp—
splashing laughter—discovering sense
in river ripples over smooth jewel clarity—
under water white otters swimming
into my reaching hands—mastering
ability in their own strengths—balancing
the body exploring knowledge, drifting
slippery currents in stream's flow, together
toward Lake Tahoe deep blue—

Crystal Range

Lily Lake trailhead
   chill clear morning—
      Slap!
Beaver dives
   under lily pads
      and rippling mountains—
crouch, splash face
   reflection scatters—
boots on granite.

      *   *   *

Beyond Glen Alpine's
   cabin dreams
sloughing necessity's
   maintenance
      to earth
trail forks—
   veer left
across rocky stream
   pick thimble berries
      from lime leaves—
the sweet treat:
   week day get-a-away—

      *   *   *

Marmot skitters on trail
   fur ripples

    through lodgepole
and white fir shadows—
   my whistle halts it
     to stand—
   dives into snowbrush
I study behaviors
  of neighbors.

      *   *   *

Quiet Grass Lake—
  jay raises havoc
    mallards splash-brag alarm!
chipmunk flicks
  along bark
   on fallen lodgepole
alternative routes
  make choices

      *   *   *

Cast line with hooked grasshopper
  into calm, clear Heather Lake
   chaliced in Sierra granite
with enchanted island
  in a blue universe.

Strike! Missed.
  A bigger hook
   in grasshopper.
Two bragging browns
  from undercut rock.

Real work:
   learning survival.

      *   *   *

Sitting on rock
   hot!
High over water
   sunlight glitters blue
     diving
into gold-crystal flames—
   Whoooooo-Cold!

Blue Fire

in the flame's
    ribbon rippling
        life's flesh—

skink tail
    sparking flecks
        sapphire the garden's
    dry crackling leaves—
sparkle light wave
    particles through my
        diamond facets

and the dragon's flame
    dancing my lungs'
        jeweled chasm

current's
    elemental minerals
        polishing touch stones
    in my bed rock hearth
coals glow stars
    embers swirl
        in my heart's river.

Silver King Creek: Upper and Lower Fish Valley

Moon's ripe crescent
thins west ridge silhouettes:
scarp shine—
Bark-yip coyotes yarp-howl
coming down switch
back scree slides
crossing boulder slopes
scattering yip, yarp, yarl
streak aspen camouflage
snow brush thickets
cascade granite ledges
weave pine—sage brush
across grass meadow
run prey down
encircling
mana.

Manifest!

Calls crack crisp air.
Crest line crags break light.
Yapping yarls, yar-yar-yar-yarp-yarp-yarp-
Yeeeoooowwwrrrrllllllllls—
Ritual spiral coursing
the beat of the heart
the chant of the breath

clamp teeth kill.
Renewal aria chorusing
yip-yip-yip-yar-yar-yar-yarp-yarp-yarp-
Yeeeoooowwwrrrrlllllllls

Air—ice—clear—
Aspen
Pine
Breathe—

Two Fish Stories

Its sudden tug's weight bent my fishing rod firm—
thrilled me to set hook—tighten drag precise—steer
it clear of roots and wood snags in grassy bank
undercuts, up over rocks near shallow riffles
downstream in West Carson River winding through
Hope Valley like a great serpent shimmering aspens.

In a deep pool, darkened with evening shades, its gray
shadow rises with the current—boiling—a big fish!
Centering it in current tires strength; but, it's too
sluggish to lose from line breakage of four pound
test line. I stand on the large, low boulder that turns
out the river's current forming back-eddy washout—
deep pool with undercut grass bank— beige in
October's chill: a soft waft of evening breeze; rock
jutted pine slopes abstract—aspens thicken dark
glitter angles; angels in clouds over peak—
a sunset to remember.

Sluggishly, its tail swirls rippled surface; it rolls on its
side, helpless in the current, skimming surface—
silvery-green-pink sheens flashing. Too huge to
inhabit this slight fall's flow. Its struggle slackened
too soon to shake the #12 gold egg hook set delicately
loose in thin, torn, twisted lip skin. I tow it into the
slow eddy as it wiggles and swims—pull it out up
sand slope to grass bank, flopping huge fish. Pink-
silver-green-rosy cutthroat, orange slash under
gulping gills.

I grab it firm in two hands to hold its struggle and squirm; a large fish: two feet long at least, but thin. Its bulk lanky, loose skinned—sudden absurdity embarrasses me. I look about for others watching the landing of this huge fish. No others watch. Two cars, a pickup and a camper passing over the river's bridge, back and forth through obvious minimal events of the river's quiet swirling over its landscape; heavy sunlight richens behind Red and Steven's Peaks— vermilion clouds gild sky.

Sense stuns me. Desperate gills, its target eye stares into awe. My hunger grips tighter. I hold it upright, belly to the ground. Rap knife spine hard on head— kills it quick—quivering still, slit vent to gills across pectorals, snip gill joint from jaw. All pulls out clean when thumb's down throat; grip gill joint, pull back organs; rinse blood vein along spine clean. Flesh is whitish-gray, soft. Cut open stomach and intestines—examine undigested food. This fish's guts empty; place guts under bush. I hook my index finger in its jaw and carry it to my car at the bridge. The clear, rich alpenglow in Hope Valley's surrounding mountain peaks—chilly.

I drive home to South Shore, Tahoe with food; the family provider's privileged meal: farmed fish fed processed meat meal, animal by-products, insect meal, synthesized, chemically balanced diet, greatest growth enhancers allowable by law, anti-biotic inoculation protection, drugged, spewed into river's wild trophy fish program. Growing thinner, non-sustainable, won't last winter, released to catch from rivers, hooked meat: semen from the world's technology.

I cook it: bar-b-que with lemon, wine, garlic and parsley sauce improves taste that's flat, soft, watery. We speak of the fish as we eat it; to retain its memory, eat it all. Still with us, part of our lives; we share our luck, skill or design? My turn in line? Reeling them in one after another, fish, fisheries fished out: our generation's harvest.

*   *   *   *

I'll tell you a fish story my memory holds true in a river's gorge. A deep pool in jammed angels curving to smooth ledges. Lodgepole, ponderosa and great cedars in bracken fern, hollow flats backed up by boulder walls crumbling centuries into minerals. Up granite slopes pines gnarl out stark fissures, accumulating soil for the eon's acid niche; saplings, snow-bent; aspen vein up north slope: black-white in violet weathered granite talus with green-gold glow in morning air.

I approach the long, curving pool below me, fifty yards long, following fault crack curve down granite boulder slope—bedrock rippling into canyon gorge. Early morning light brightens broken ridge line above; cracked column walls falling into a glacier's slide of pure stone. Air chills near water—narrowing rush slash arcs off incline, crystal slice splashes, rolls into trough widening out ledge pool level—lapping thin sheets riffling off round granite to slick rock mist pools—rocky spouts pour—churn froth spills, boils—swirls—licks light rippling across large, dark pool, clear as mind's memory tumbling gravel to sandy bottom shore gathering wood debris. Farther out, glassy.

A deep pool, sharp shaped boulders on bottom, it widens out large ledge of river's staircase into gorge's roar. Dark emerald shade of boulders and lodgepoles along pool's east edge. An evening moon's crescent shape, the pool's white water horn turns back descending white-gray, broken granite boulders to bedrock ribs shattering dark silk crystal images-pulsing-sliding like snake scales of great serpent: terror and beauty—jay squawk-squach-screeches: aaaack! aaaack!

Sunlight on snowbrush and willows along west edge of pool. Lodgepole scatter out on flat across river in a hollow. Still dark water; light mist off surface shimmers stone mantra: Diamond Sutra drips over all—sun's intensity at eastern rim fractures across clear, cold electricity. I approach it.

A powerhouse size boulder turns the current's white water spilling into the pool. On the lee side, a sand and mud bank supporting brushy willows and a few young aspen—one snap-crushed under a five foot wide, squared erratic from the cliff's face—last year's spring or winter.

I stand on grasses growing into water—to my right, roots under bank cut. A submerged log with spines off shore, six feet deep, along the base of this fifteen foot diameter, under cut boulder on my left. In its shadow, in a small clearing, enough room with strength and skill, to land a hooked fish, I prepare to cast.

The cascade's froth flowing toward me, the pool's current flowing away from me, the roar flowing through me—within it, I cast out far: thirty yards across current, downstream into river's glassy, dark, deep flow—the line falling, floating. I reel in slack, feel tug of lure action. Mepps spinner #2; shiny silver in sunlight; jig it a bit—ride swirls, natural-like over—Strike! Hard. Set hook. Drag whirrrrrrrrrs-line downstream—crank reel, tighten drag, crank faster—line's spray light zips cross current. Rod bent, quivering fish runs to foot of pool's rapids.

I tighten drag, pull rod over to my right, curving fish back upstream into current but line slackens in slow side current of deep water. I jerk rod back overhead, reeling slack—fish swims strong toward root bank. I swing rod out to current, reeling; fish bolts across current—breaks-surface jumping golden-shaking throe—tail dancing out of light—-plunges dark satin swirl of deep current. Huge fish! Leaps light spray shaking, twisting spasm—slap-splash to shake hook. Taut line in water's angle anchors its jaw joint—fragile—keep line firm-soft. Slack or jolts shakes it or breaks it loose.

Strong, vibrant—rod quivering heavy staccato tug. I guide it back into current, reeling upstream, tiring its strength. Quick run tugs strong into river's current. Sudden dash toward me slackens line. I lift rod high, still tight line, reel faster. Fish swims toward roots under bank; lean out far left, rod tip turns it toward log—bolting down to the log but no strength to tangle line on log's spines; fish muscles into froth of deep rapids—runs out twenty yards tiring. I feel it strong and heavy in my line, reel and rod—drag it tighter—bring it back toward me off center of fast current into slower water of the pool's back current between root bank and the rock with submerged log; then, with luck, up through grasses to shore line ten inches deep in drop off. How will I land such a big fish?

The fish image forms as it swims closer, breaks surface; color flash thrills—huge fish! Not quite caught. But this close is enough. This fish and I—I will eat it if I catch it. I believe it knows this. First sight of me scares it down to log; then, out to current. It rolls in the white water—bright shimmer, huge body thrashing tail, slap-splash, dives curves back toward root bank. I turn it with rod tip back into swift heavy water, tire its violent thrashings to shake loose-tight hook out of its jaw's joint; steer it back toward me between snags near shore among lush grasses.

It darts back out—I reel steady—bring it back in close among the grasses and step left foot into water. It darts out, circles, swirling surface. I'm reeling slower, lift rod in right hand, arching over my head, steering fish steady, reach down with left hand—jam thumb into throat—grab lower jaw. It bites tight. I haul it out as lure falls from jaw. Fish shakes, vibrates desperate. I step back from shore into clean, white river stones and grasses among snowbrush. A big fish, hard, strong body, firm, sleek muscled, bronzy-silver antique hue: Brown Trout, orange circles like Jupiters burning in its body—beautiful, struggling to free itself.

On its side, in dark green grass among white-silver, smooth granite boulders, I look into its eye. This fish: pure life, perfect body and spirit—praise it and kill it quick—preserve flavor. Belly down on rich grass; hard raps on skull—a fish tail emerges from its throat. I pull out a Rainbow, eight inches, still bright, fresh swallowed. I lay it aside. I hold the big Brown on its back—twenty-one inches long a full girth. My knife slitting up belly pressures second fish tail out of mouth. Another Rainbow, eight inches, fresh swallowed—three fish in one! Fish of wisdom.

I clean the big Brown, quivering in my hands as I cut out blood vein along backbone; nervy, it nearly slips back into the current out of sight. German Brown Trout: voracious eater of Rainbows. Bright orange-pink flesh: firm muscle, deep red blood, male glands—blood of rhythm in the river's roar. Good, honorable and wild on my tongue. I lift its water to my lips, cupped in my hands and drink—smell pure food in my hands; thank the river for its fruit of wisdom. Cut two smaller fish—firm, pink flesh inside, best flavor—rich, wild trout from the great serpent's body!

Three more days I travel down the canyon exploring its wild terrain. Eat all three fish. On the third day, I climb out up wall of main fork canyon. At sunset, crossing a snow bank below the last rim, I cross over the ridge and start down slope between lava columns—clouds fiery rose. I walk trail of shadows through waxing moon's glow among fir, lodgepole, skunk cabbage to my car. Drive home to South Shore Lake Tahoe's glittering lights.

What's the Matter

"What's the matter," he says, tying on
the deer hair hackle fly that hour tied,
"don't you have any sporting blood in you?"

"Hell no," I answer, inserting the gold barbed
hook into the grasshopper that hour caught
gently, to preserve its fat, tender body
"killing ain't no game!"

Tenaya Canyon

I wake—dark shades: twilight—cedar and pine spice me. Out of my sleeping bag—speckled sky in thick forest lightens Mirror Lake still, reflects trees, rock, sheer—stars fade—twizzzle bird. Scratching in pack sack—squirrel ransacks it, jitter chortles flees with my last raisin muffin, clenched in its teeth, leaping along old fallen cedar trunk—I chase; but, can only laugh. It disappears into forest brush between big, speckled, granite boulders.

Tenaya Canyon: glacier scraped stone of Half Dome's mirror image. Water's stone crevasse! Sand settles lake's shape returning to a stream: Tenaya Creek.

Similar, in a sense, to the old ones who vanished into the stone's glare between known and unknown worlds—entropy? Disturbance in the undergrowth—shape-flick-vague—passing into deeper shades chink of rock! Something is alive out there, moving things, camouflaged in growth and decay, long before the Yosemites, fleeing the invaders into their sacred power of stone's elements.

I splash my face in chilly reflection. All there is—here! Culmination cupped in my hands—the bluish crystal glows in this stone's expanse splashing my face at lake edge. Sand, gathering willows; pines clump closer; lost Mirror Lake fills with minerals rippling eons—black oak leaves—breathe deep.

I eat oatmeal, raisins, honey cereal; soaked apricots; almonds and brazil nuts; rainbow trout cooked at Florence Lake night before last. Now, the hike out up Tenaya Canyon; search for a passage to the white stone's light in sapphire: Lake Tenaya—Py-wee-ack!

I roll up sleeping bag; stuff pack; fix all parts secure. Light pack fifth day out from June Lakes, Cathedral Peak, Florence Lake, down the Merced; thick, heavy sand in Little Yosemite; the twin falls roar into the sheer valley's air.

From Mirror Lake, I'll follow water closely, searching for openings; listen to the water spill and rush. But the din of tourists increases with sunlight; their anxious desires smoke morning air toxic; the great granite canyon walls magnify—clashing of their metals drowns the low gurgling of the stream's flow into its clear reflection—jay squacks—chipmunk chatters.

I flee the invasion, follow deer, bear and coyote: ancient indigen trails under oak canopy far below the sunlit rim. Canyon, live and black oak forest; cedar and pine intersperse up steep slopes. I climb through snow brush, manzanita, over rock outcrops—gnats buzz about my face, into eyes, ears, nose, down throat in deep breath—cough! Hack it up out of throat: spit it or eat it. Protein!

At Snow Creek, the canyon narrows; it's hot, sweaty in sun. I search for clues: angle of incline, grip of surface, tree and brush slopes, route of Yosemites in their spirit's terrain—the wise ones among ancient stones—passing through this landscape's reverence—water and wind of their lives.

I climb outcrops and talus slides when open, big boulders and ledges to the stream's interior, looking for the guides in its mystery: up the staircase waterfall pools into the sanctuary's passage—the body moves instinct's skill.

I switchback up steep north slope, brushy, scattered trees; gnats bug me here. Heat rises up slope to rock walls too sheer to climb out. I hike across brushy rock outcrops to a granite prominence to view a passage across the canyon's stream. Where would one escape here?

Canyon of hanging valleys. Far below, to my left, a flat, dry riverbed interspersed with pines and cedars. The creek disappears in the rocks and gravels—emerging at the bedrock's cascade leaps into lower valley a steeper slope of flow, disappearing under thick oak, pine and cedar canopy: velvety, like algae in a stone crevice, but immense.

And where the clear stream flows hidden, below me, microscopic in the canyon's huge, green, dense cleft, a single gray rock! It is a large rock—pebble-like from his height—an oval, egg-like speck in a green frothy abstraction: a nebula among bluish-gray light shafts into a chasm's womb.

What I am looking for, I find! On my left, up at the creek's highest drop, white Pywackit Cascades plunge into blue-deep pool; a crystal thread flows from it through a level valley—drops three high, thin ribbon falls off three large, bedrock ledges cradling emerald pools: three grottoes—lovely as any sacred chamber could be, ferns and flowers gushing from high, arching, circular walls.

Below the fourth drop's rocky cascade, a wide, smooth, whitened ledge holds a pool. Big, white boulders piled up to it on near side allow crossing to climb a young pine to a narrow incline ledge up to a steep, narrow crack curving up granite dome face into sapphire.

On my right, beyond Half Dome, far down in the under story of Yosemite's deepest canyon, flowing through it, the tourist roar hums; smoke and smog cloud the immense present. Minimalist: blue, green and rock! Far down in the protoplasmic green sea of leaves below me the oval stone, perhaps an embryonic touchstone—a microcosm. What is time in this cleavage of rock?

Sudden disturbance! Movement at the edge of the egg shaped gray stone in the primordial green froth below me. Sienna, reptilian shapes, lizard-like from this height, crawl out of the green of trees, circling clockwise up the stone— like a tower—above the trees. Two humans, naked, crawl into the rock's nucleus-like center, embrace: legs and arms entwine, one to another, facing each other, become one, like chromosomes in the canyon's genetic flow: softly, like riffles in the leaves and the hidden stream, their cries of love rising—falling in the canyon's still, clear light.

Michie Peak Myth
for R. P. & G. S.

From Cherry Creek walk south
up rock ledges—between Twin Lakes
up Michie Peak's west ridge—out of conifers.
Shale-like rubble, rectangled fractured
fragments stick up sharp on ridge spine flat.
Shattered rock cradles nine crystal pools—
Green velvet moss, lush grass embroidery
tarn-like pool, shallow—spring marsh?

Pause to drink, crouched—in black sand/mud.
Print! Fresh—one, maybe two days—
lion drank here—male or female, huge!
I have knife. No desire to prove or protect.
Move over ridge down sloped boulder jumble—
into granite's gash—odor. Pungent meat rot.
Carcass—deer! Three days old? Head missing
meat and fur on bones, greasy—drying—
guts gone, flies buzz hollow—hot sun.

Switch back down granite debris ledges
to glacial cleft between ridge hips.
Hooves beat earth under pines—
through brush, between trunks
four does, two bucks, more, drum
out of mountain garden—a shadow! Wings
passing through light shafts piercing canopy
burst brilliant needles—eagle—golden

curving over Michie Peak's south ridge thigh—
gone! Deer hooves fade in white granite gulf—

Red Tail lifts out of pines—circling west—
I move under old conifers into pink-scarlet
florescence—paintbrush flames undulate radiance.
Thick, dark, green heather's white flower foam
brims the scarlet pool, oval for one-hundred yards
then steep, white cliffs, five-hundred feet up
form crotch of two ridges, slick silver/white thighs
enclosing this floral bowl—aroma
pools blood's hunger for elixir!

Vertical, tree lined slit splits
mountain's hips, scarlet oval meets it
at passage to naked belly granite up Michie Peak—
but, near its scarlet oval's apex, a tawny shape
lithe, threading bush, rock, slit, gone!
I turn from its molten field's nectar—
the life force hums intensity—ascend
the low rise, following the others—
What wild eyes watch this human
vanish?

Graces in Yosemite

Dawn water
          slashes slate rock
  emerald rippling moss
    fish swirls
silver lure   splashing
          slippery brook trout
  in skillet   sizzles
    crisp   firm   warm
good!

        *   *   *   *

Hike up north face slope Kerrick Canyon
          red fir
  groundsel   yarrow   corn lilies
    swallow doe and fawn
      in light shaft
  through hemlock shadows
canyon slope steepens
          up duff trail
  switch backs
    rocky tumbling creek
      flashing crystal
  narrow canyon deep
aspen glitter
          at ridge pass
  boulders stand tall
    like lodgepoles
      quiet

      cracked granite
emerald tarns

         *   *   *   *

South face slope steep down
        switch back
                rock decays
breaks

      turns under boot
          slip

snowbrush   manzanita   stiff   thick
      skin hot   dusty
           blood crusts gouge
eyebrows dazzle light
      clear cold stream slits trail
           kneel   splash face   drink
crouched

         *   *   *   *

Dusky slate-like
      granite peaks
          drop fault blocks
      into lodgepole forest
east end of valley
      west end Benson Lake sapphire
          scramble down outcrop
      glacier moraine
walk through bracken fern to long grass sprays

                pine thin to aspen   cool breeze
                         crystal flared waves
                splashing golden sand
granite glacier shine

                *   *   *   *

Sit against white smooth log
          in warm sand
                    thin grass   willows
                zephyrs
      eat apricots   almonds   raisins
laughter flickering through air
          long hair flowing
                    bronzed   three women
                run   naked
     between willow clumps
on sapphire

               sparkling
                         wavelets
                    reaching
          for a gold
disk—

Blue Earth

Granite slabs
    avalanche the crystals'
        ecstatic laughter—-
basalt's liquid tongues
    cascade the cliff's teeth

and the Sierra's red earth
    marbles blue stone veins
        to ocean's heart beat

fire rippling the wilderness
    and the waves' flames
        leap from the prophet's tongue
as sand rivulets sift shapes
    pattern the landscape's brilliance

the watershed's flesh
    channels stone into blue clay
        shaping our vessel's worth.

The Vessel

Opening the eye's Iris
    shapes clay's
        substantial weight:
elegant—simple line
    eloquent—curve
        form fits—Grace
governing function:
    the thing

nature nurtures
    creates real value—
        holds collective space:
each and all
    volume worthy
        in relationship—
what it means:
    the thing

alpine lake alpenglow
    granite lipped, still, hemlocks
        silhouette lavender air
the silver talus ridge arêtes
    aflame in full moon
        rising—reflection
deepening lake's
    dark-clear-depth

imagination
    envisioning light chalice
bone radiates.

Yosemite – Le Conte Lodge Ecology Poetics
Moon When Sunlight Drips From Leaves

We gather
   in granite sanctuary:
      bell centered dome—
Sierra cut blue granite
   block masoned walls—
      first cut coast redwood
      timbers arch support.
All that work to get here—
   Nature's minds
      rest in their place—
   reverent light fills—
Thunder heads mushroom
   over alpine angels' home—
      silent sky—splits
distant lights crack.
   rumble where the clouds rest
      on shoulders of granite memorials.

You got to get good gear.
   Take a hike all day
      or a week—better—more.
What senses experience
   write feeling flashes—observations
      research—character—
   imagination plays between—
What's taken in—pack it out.
   what thought—show how.
      All relates with self.

      Revision—Inspiration.
Real work.

Take a long route home—
    rest stop frequent—
        investigate landscape character.
    Listen—let sand speak.
Up silver-white crystal highway
    Tenaya Lake blue: light chalice—
      granite domes glow polished
    clouds pearl—
luminescent expressions
    adorn templed walls—
      light columns gild reliefs—
Should I metaphor Michelangelo?

Iced edged wind caresses
    will to be here—
Lightning bolts invigorate
    Tioga Pass apex
ragged rock tears clouds
    ice chisels sentiment
      lessons etched in granite text.
    Need I metaphor Moses?
The mind's eye
    snaking terror chasm
      carves eastern Sierra's
    manifest destiny—
survival is reverence.

At Mono Lake
    grebes pattern millennium lay over

       navigate mirage suspensions
into abstract silver scene
   sailing quantum hieroglyphics
     brine shrimp define the algal maze
among tufa silhouettes:
   salt figures dissolving their sins.
Evangelists prepare us for such dearth:
   lowest common denominator
     stains lake lower
   at south state stand off.
In a wicked, evil world
   sooner the better—chosen
buying up heaven's gates.

Meanwhile, money lenders bet stats
   in nuclear heat: bury it deep
Perfect petty debates
   defer final solution:
     dilution of pollution.
   Don't drink the water—-
dry sophistication:
   searing wind's dust veils
     teasing the desert's remnants—-
   ghosts of their deeds.
At perception shift's
   scenic view point
circle in closer
   there's money to be made
     splitting hair's atom—-
   cluck and cackle weather reports
put up the stakes—signs
   too many tourists here.

Get down
   in sage brush rock.
We lunch on cataclysmic glass
   rim of earth's porous progress:
      Panum Crater.
Watch pyrotechnic celestials
   enliven language discussion:
      graphic exchanges smoldering
ozone spirits dancing—lightning strikes
   the blue vault's granite spine—-
details tracing white hot nerve
   leaping precipitous peaks
      sparking granite—andesite—basalt.
Connecting points charging
   northern peak incline.
We pack up—take auto trail
   to ozone hot spot springs
      following sky dragon's
spent scent seen over sage.

At Bridgeport portal
   classic Sawtooth Ridge
      to Matterhorn Peak
cloaked in pearl-purple opulence
   white rock crowns
      glacial retreats—-
green rich cattle field spreads
   global warming methane
      stereotypical wild west image:
   dude ranch cowboys
and their cowgirls ride——-
   What was it really like?

    Sierra sunset round up
   corralling buck's reality:
geophysical cost in narrow focus—-
     winning the west: subsidize iron rails
        petroleum technology—nuclear
     fission—split Nature:
two edged sword!

II

Up Robinson Creek's moraine valley
    in sage brush, Jeffrey pine, aspen—
        trailing golden ribbons from rock flanks
flickering September chill—
    the springs we drink from.
In debris of Holocene wash outs
    boulder and sand mounds
       glacial erratics
elements of a good camp site
    out of wind and the creek cold draft
       on flat, under pine
    in Sierra showers—cool
view: all passing—

Lightning! Blazing
    scars ridge spike cream
       thunder drum shakes.
Azure nugget jay
    squaaaaaaaachks at us.
So, we drink green tea
    under large Jeffrey pine
       vanilla-pineapple aroma

     furrowed coconut cream nose gay
a few pine nuts cracked
   from scattered cones—
sage in the storm's aura
    since we first arrived
       and before us, the others—
   the ancient ones
in survival's search for the good life.

Stove in sand heats water to boil.
    Post modern fire keeper tool:
       easy—danger in its power.
We have come to this:
    huddled under the lone pine
       in the storm's enchantments—
moraine's white granite
   oblique geometric
      sand grain shifting epoch—-
   stone age—
smudged in wet sage—
   a rainbow jewels
      desert peaks to the east—
brief flutter of yellowing aspens
   showers gold—
      crystal chill.
Lightning—ozone caress—

In boiling water steam—
   Shape! Black
     in silver-white sand.
Arrow Point—notched triangle:
   obsidian—surface worn, old

two edged blade.
    Tip's curve cut-rips
        perfect into flesh
    to break and fester—
What story can it tell?
    Does it matter
        or just curiosity
Utility art work
    or relic of the way?
Dissolving dark matter—
    Lightning Strikes!

Pilgrimage

Snake up steep Highway 89 hair-pin turns—
    no guard rails here—fire scars
        pinion, Jeffrey pine to white fir—
    clear air escarp—breathe—
Walker/Carson divide—
    high desert sage panoramas—
        north/south ranges align deep valleys:
    stone waves rising—folding crumpled earth—
Sierra sight seeing—Monitor Pass: 8300 ft.
    Stop—check it out.

Boiled elemental soup slopped
    up from plate skid's continental drift—
        Tertiary basalt crust—granite pluton's
    sharp peaks break up
glaring polished form: beauty-raw—
    the Garden's abstract flowers
        recent snow streamers crystallize
    glacial slick crest gem rock shining—
cobble and gravel alluvial etch facets
    angling jeweler's eye
        down white ice zone cleavage—
    Mesozoic building block hips
split landscape lava—
    east—west snow melt minerals
        filter balancing act: acid
    alkaline—elemental exchanges
nourishing resident developments:
    golden aspen groves

    heirs of their soil's roots
  all one in community—lifting limbs
over spring's dried flowers—fruit and seeds—
  available space between natives—

Juniper fracture October light
  on prominent look outs—tough
    old growth triple trunk giant at pass
  spire's centuries—three spared crown—
dynamics of exchanging fluids—
  its fiber connection spans sky-earth energy
    dancing across lava ridge's spines—
Deities we imagine—electrifying
hogbacks—dike edge seams glowing—
  lightning bolts charging Round Top's dome
    magnify crest aura
  shimmering light down
pine needle thighs: striding north
  in watershed's immaculate flesh.

Raw ingredients shape shifting:
  geologic positioning—PH factor
    enzymes in molecular magnetism
  genetic fiber and flesh matrix
intertwining white water generations
  nourishing river arms' energy—
    twist-flux current muscles
  our palms' potency washed clean
pooling the Great Basin sinks
  with millennium expose:
    giardia—mercury—cyanide
  perchlorates—plutonium—gamboling—

    the wet mirage in thin air—
        can you really get it while you can?

Thunder heads richen—
    mountain sage brush bristles—
        rabbit brush sulfur swaths volcanic
    lichen murals on fire black igneous
intrusions: organic/inorganic sculpture
    defines sage curved plane—
        Mutualism art image
    Sacrament under the tongue—
enzymatic musings in primordial lime
    orange, red, rust lichen simplicity—
        food for thought's clarity—
    contact points affecting senses:
attachment to others—
    all of our relationships evolving
        exchanging influences between bodies
    quivers possibility becoming real—

The fall wind scythe shivers us
    rattles sky blue iris's death mask over the field—
        purple pentstemon skeletons
    murmur seeds into rivulet dust devils
smoking the summit sage brush range—
    high in meadows of seeps and springs
        the aspen grove's gold pleasures:
    ephemeral leaves flickering
light points filtering golding leaves—
    groves of the old growth giants
        limbs in the wind's presence:
    the millennium hymn evolving

their cymbals' prophetic design:
    to live is to flutter together—
        in the white walled glen's epiphany:
    sanctuary of Holy—
we open our arms to It's showering light.
    Alive! Being Here in It's atmosphere
        misting Reynold's Peak: spiked crest
    altar flaming jeweled clouds.

Twilight crossing the range's gold
    white brevity in sweet grasses warmth—
        the camp fire aura pulsing
blue-lavender-gold-silver-orange
petaling our bodies—circling
    it's heat flame—making ritual—dancing
        the golden leaves blessing flames—
    sage in the cool night breathing—
we lie down with the harvest
    in each other's arms:
        our redemption's kiss.
Holiest Holy Breathing over our bodies
our cries of love rising in leaves' applause—
    chilly raindrops sparking skin laughter
        gold leaves falling in the breathing of the
breeze—
    in the archetype fire licking leaves—falling
sparking—sizzle: air-water-earth-fire

In star lit clouds silvering the changes—
    in the leaves' veils in the wind's assurance
        owl hooting moon rise into clouds
    coyote barks sharp—howls

the Garden's fire glows—
    animal repose in our Nature—leaves
      falling year after year—coinage
  in our passage: flesh into Earth—
our particles in subterranean springs
    in It's clear light—our lives
      in this landscape our love embraces.
Here, we open arms to It All—

Comets

Five days after
Yosemite Valley reopens—
river's beautiful devastation
reclaiming the old ways
in a ripple through an era's tide—
April Christens the valley:
indigo clouds fuel sunset
rain veils' fire.
Granite ignites!

The day's last light gone.
Drive home through dark
canyon shapes curve up mountain
around ridge rock—over
into forest enclosure—
down—blind turn—

Enormous!
Canyon black void opens.
Strange tint of moonlight rising
behind Sierras coronas crest line crystal.
The bright comet flares northwest
perfect above horizon—soon gone!
Never again in our lives—
How can we value that
in wondrous lights of space?

To comfort lack in immensity
dropping into canyon, steep, dark

narrow winding road, pull off slow
onto shoulder at cliff edge—stop!
Turn off headlights, engine, set brake.

Soon, full moon over the ridge
above us.
We step into galactic star fire—
Breathe the cool breeze—moist.

Meteor streak!
Hidden moon—strange glow silvering
ridge lines etching before us—
Toulumne—Stanislaus—American.
What value this space we share?

Cliff edge falls into river's rush-roar
muffles millions of years carving deeper—
dark around us—no human light—
balmy whispers cliff chaparral—

The comet's crystal veil
blessing Andromeda and Perseus
guiding us home among these stars—
atoms of a universe—
swirling our Milky Way flesh—
Warm with each other
loving one another
breathing the wind's ridge pines—
the full moon rising—eclipsed!
In black pearl glow we kiss—

Blue Breeze

In blue breeze shimmering
    afternoon Aprils
        the garden's deep green—
fiber lava bone swells
    bubbling juices
        mineral stew's raw flesh—

snakes slithering its wilderness
    salmon leap crystal education
        following the monologue:
syllables gathering relationships
    in the sacred drum pounding
        grounding this body's rituals—

in the place of being real
    a smoke wisp
        unfurls
over marsh reeds—
    up the great river's magnificent arms
        ocean whispering its language—

Yuba Mother Gold
with Jacquie & Claire

Water wildfire shoots
    granite canyon—
rocks balance difference
    between gold metal
        and fall's big leaf maple—

Kissing stone altars
    imprint our passing murmur
        in willow ripple—
white leaves whirling sky dream
    sparkle light wave-particles
        across current clear emerald—

Swirling crescendo
    echoing through arteries:
        deep swell flow—
Oh, Primordial Mother
    we come—

Visitation

Sometimes I am a chosen witness
for miracles appearing among mundane.
Male nudes in primal manhood
hangout at the river—ten all-tan guys
lounging on rocks—standing—talking
among the big boulders around
intimate sand beach at emerald pool
where Yuba River sculpts images
in millennium theme's white granite.

We all see her coming—across
the river, walking towards us—the way
she moves arouses our raw exposure—
short shorts, loose blouse—fluff hair
and with her small boy friend/lover—
her features like a model's—or goddess!
Up on the flat top rock stage above us.
She unzips her shorts, lets them fall
from her shapely maiden hip nuance—
unbuttons her blouse—it slides from
her golden brown shoulders, breasts
thighs—fiery blond hair glowing
the ripe body of woman's essence.

Four men dive in and swim upstream
escaping the rising heat in their flesh—
two turn to excuse, rock scramble away.
Three retreat into big boulders
among shady crevices in urine stink

shy, dress quickly, murmur in shadows.
I, alone, am left naked at water's edge—
She dives like an arrow sent from the forest
wild into the emerald pool—then she rises
a gold-crystal veil falling from her hair
shoulders, breasts, arms, hips, her thighs—
illuminating her naked aura's flame—
laughter in her lips—ripples swirl round
her ankles: diamonds in river emerald!

Two arm lengths from me, She smiles
rose wet cheeks and lips—almond eyes
flashing river mystery—
She turns, calls to her young lover/friend
"Take your clothes off! C'mon, dive in!"
He shakes his head, squats upon the rock
watching her, scared young man that he is—
alone among the men to defend her.
I recognize such fear in me—aroused
in awe of her presence, touchable—
I could not speak till asked—neither
if I, he, take my pants off in exposure
hard-on saluting the radiant sun, flowering
the sweet scent of her sex. I could
name her; but, She knows her own name!

What glowing brilliance in her face.
Perhaps a goddess—who owns authority
to assess such judgments? She giggles
glories in satisfaction: nude woman being
alone among men—untouchable in her power—

too much to behold in the rock arena's maledom.
She dives into the emerald pool—disappears
downstream—I am alone on the sand shore
her Visitation a memory among the men.

River Dance

To learn the dance
    you gotta go down
        to the edge
            the river—
Go ahead
    it's all right.
        Touch it!
Nice body.   Huh!
    It moves—
Hold that water flesh
    in your fingers—
        uh-huh—you got it!
Take off your clothes—Yea—
    Oh Yea!   Slip in
        naked and—slow—
Feel that soft spot
    OOOOOOOOO-between your metaphors—
That's right—let go
    touch it all over.
Swim in rhythm
    in that river's current.
Be aware.   Sensitive.
    Each nuance
        read true.
Go with it
    ride what you learn.
Don't trash your lover's life!
    Keep your stream clean.
        Pure—
You know what I mean.

River Festival

The blue sky
ribbon rippling
our Mother's chasm

Cascades granite
into my emerald's
deep soul pool

Her serpent scent
slithers up my
chakra cartilage

    *

Boulders roar
Her kundalini jewelry

Bedrock energy
silvers our staircase

Clear crystal
quivers April leaves

    *

Revival salmon
spawn scarlet
flames—pearl
my riffled lungs'
gravel—

Down By the Yuba
— *Things To Do* –

Hey, hey, all day
I could stay
down by the Yuba
   in sunlight
   swimming emerald pools
   staying cool
   hot on polished stone
     with pretty girls
     Ohhh—their sexy curls
     like river swirls
        or scrambling over boulders
        I want my body in tune
        lift rocks and muscle shoulders
        my honey rubs in summer's moon.

Hey, hey, all night
bright star light
down by the Yuba
   a rising moon
   with a crackling fire
   ahhhh—desire
   dancing round the flames
     my pretty girl's
     delicate twirls
     her skirt unfurls
        laughing at coyote's howl
        on sand, warm, in love—peace

      sleep————————shriek of owl!
    breathe deep in the dawn's increase.

Hey, hey, all day
we can play
or soak in the sun
   roasting skin
   meditate like tree
   sing lark free
   in the wildflowers
      the gold's perfume
      my heart, it blooms
      howls at the moon
         dive—naked with God—baptize
         sheer canyon walls guide me through
         the rapids wild—cleanse my eyes
         pray to God—I sing it true!

Hey, hey, all day
we can play
down at the Yuba!

Camouflage

Thin trail dusty—
    steep canyon plunge
whitewater, emerald pools:
    Yuba River—
Laurel scent sweetens
    tannin
        in canyon oak grove.
Here
    I search for stuff
        of poems.

White paper litter
    flutters
        under laurel bough
just off trail
    about to slip
        down
loose gravel-granite slope—

I stop
    to pick it up
        wait—
dark, red-brown shit
    smeared on it—
a turd slide—
    slithers from
        under it
twists back up—jumps—
    alligator lizard snaps
a black fly's flight
    from the shit smear!

Stepping Out

December clouds cold all day—
    after Christmas clean up, inside
        here to there arrangements
    what we do with our lives—passing
till evening light instills
    landscape pastels golden—
        yellow pine, fir, cedar abstract
    up Deer Creek Canyon ridge lines
into Banner Mountain highlights:
    angels pearl vermilion gold
        lavender air—twilight fades
    our dark room enamels
flickering-flames-quiet—
    shadowing darkness—withering time
        approaching midnight—
    right place
right moment.

We just stood up
    walked out the door
        into cold breeze brilliance—
    inhale the night—stars
pulsing mythic constellations
    our senses enliven:
        Sirius blazing blue, red crystal
    through lace veil—falling
over Sierra crest—
    down the horned owl's pine-oak ravine
        who-whooo whoo   whoo

    ffffwweeeeeee, ffffwwweeeeeee, ffffwwweeeeeee
wood ducks splashing pond
    chasing positions among stars
        in full moon wane
    nearing apex—at its height!
Mars so close: sperm to egg
    in galaxy's winter cold—
        blue oak limbs uplifting praise
    the moment we enter—
hoooootle—hoooootle—hoooootle—

Flaming—double edged meteor
    white-gold-scarlet piercing
        Moon—Mars—extinguished—
    in heavenly body of whales—
brighter than we have seen before
    glowing implications
        in divining stars
    spiraling our circles
in this birth of our eyes
    how many return?   aarrrah
        aarrrah,   aarrrah,   aarrrah —-
    from the dark matter question—
circumferenced in moon halo
    silhouettes glide—pearl nucleus
        reflecting—obsidian pool
    rippling imagination through winter
night light—we breathe—

Decide:
    step out into the dark
        much more often—

Toward Evening

A pale thin line penetrates sunlight
    up Deer Creek's dark green canyon
flying low, her-honk, her-honk, her-honk—
    geese, turn north
        rising with forest slope
            over Peaceful Valley
along east edge of this promontory
    point of migration
sunlight still on their wings' steady thrust up—
    once, a few years ago
        never again as large a flock
            four thousand—

In three great rippling waves
    far off, southwest
        I heard their quibbling
    rolling melody of syllables
arriving and rising
    counterclockwise into a circle
        upon a circle and another circle
    in a gyre's vortex, pulsing
above me, in its axis
    my mind whirling wild
        in this milky swirl of stars—
    then off—north—
and the next flock arriving, circling
    and rising as before into its
        three ringed spiral above me
    in its greatest loft, afloat

in the up draft—still—
    gathering its body
        for the great pulse of wings
    and off—
and the third flock arriving—circling
    rising in its widening spiraling circle:
        a double helix of wings—complete
    the generations continuing—

As these few now continue up slope
    twenty-three Canadian Geese confirmed:
        an arrow's repose, humming energy
    in this perfect arc of wings
between the Gray Pines'
    massive forked limbs' needles of light
        in lavender sky—
    whooooogh   whooooogh   whooooogh
wings over my head into vermilion
    flaring the Blue Oak gold
        gnarled on rock ridge!

Native Cypress

Three weeks hard rain!
Nailing coffin lid
on cabin fever sweats—
couldn't take it!

Walked out into its drizzle
up Newtown Road side
into Macnab Cypress grove
stood under gray-green
fountains—clean, wet aroma—
new year's first sunshine
over pine velvet canyon—
Deer Creek's roar!

Puzzled

At Bridgeport Park
                scarlet splashes
     lush green grasses
                   dew wet—

On pine bark
             pieces
    scattered
                  blood globs—

Star thistle
             skeletons
     dripping blood
              pools—

Alive
            Lady Bird Beetles
    in January sunshine
               buzz—

Animal Grace

I gave up race, phone, electricity
    to care-take wood frame cabin
        open windows all around
ridge flat under
    nine ancient black oaks—
Manzanita, kit-kit-dizze heat resins
    deer bush froths flowers
lean, tall black oak, pine
    sapling raving slope
        regenerating
    gold rush clear cut—
under story
    fire in forties.

I study trails, plants, animals
    drink water from spring fed stream
        poured over my body
bathe under bright black oak leaves—
Gather sprouts, fungus, berries, flesh
    leaves changing color/shape
        decorate corner slough—

When winter sunlight captures me
    I curl into oak leaf drift till
        sunset chill—
cold nights, compose flames
    dancing
        moonlight forest—

Exchange coinages with horned owls—
   Hoooooootles with screech owls—

A bear visits regularly—we grunt!
   Between tricks
      raccoons teach laughter—
Lizards and spiders dine at sills
   occasional titmouse flutters in for tidbit.
Under golden black oak boughs, I meditate.
   Bucks, does socialize murmuring their lips
      bright teeth shelling acorns—
A golden eagle winters here
   living off rodents: cats, small dogs.

Robins, jays chorus
   finches crescendo, warbling
      flicker's clear-call-piercing—
Wasps hum, drowse me, rhapsody.

The new human neighbors don't know
   my cunning smile—
I've learned to be invisible
   thread trails through manzanita thickets
      to sunsets humans won't see
   until they look—
Howl at moonrise—coyotes harmonize
   walk dark forest path
      in cricket rhythm
   crouch on wet stone
      listen—water trickle—
Praise moon-shine cupped in hands!

Each day our hands discover

Each day our hands discover
    the blue-emerald river heart:
jewel that radiates
    the canyon's deepest image:
the forest fountain
    bubbling wilderness
down the granite crags'
    building block foundation:
our soul's precious body:
    a sweet communion for our lips—

Speaking vast secrets
    fates sing of spirits
unfurling leaves
    from golden black oaks
nourishing the lupine nectar
    rippling spring rivulets
glowing dawn fire—
    we dive into its clear pool
spirit laughing
    our river current—

River Light

in the mind—deep
    emerald pools
        granite canyon—
we reflect what is
    passing through rock
        sand grinds deeper
each year of our lives
    memories flowing
        out of sight—

we look up stream to what is
    coming—entranced
        green serpentine flow
conifers, oaks, poison oak
    mock orange and black locust
        sweeten body's electric
movement we watch—
    water bubbling rolling
        over cobbles between bedrock
splashing beauty clear
    rhythm character
        polishing gem stone
crystal cascade lace patterns
    between white bone:
        gold of our lives—
we climb naked—warm
    into marrow's
        beautiful canyon—
where this woman gathers

      her movements true
          to her course before her
in rapid's churn—roars
     the river's green-gold light
          pooling her body's treasure—

battered by the brute
     boulders' course
          to ocean's
generation—spiraling
     cycles encircling
          this world body
she becomes more beautiful
     each day widening my embrace
          to the essential element—

so it is we enter
     the jeweled pool—pleasure
          wetting imagination
embracing flesh
     in current light
          sliding over bones
rippling between boulders
     into crux of power
          coming together—frothing
cascade's ruffling rush
     salmon leaping up stream
          coming—still—quivering
flush red
     pool's last light
          mirroring
bubbling cascades
     cleansing desire

             rippling downstream
current swirls
        each day
             this woman and I
swimming upstream
        coursing the falls'
              wet light miracle—

Mining the American

Up on the north fork
dreams are still mined
dredged from the river's sand
and bottom mud
sucked out
from under jumbled boulders
bigger than dreams.

Up river
past the aggregate mine
the color ripples
like the willows
across gravel bars
four-wheel-drive mules
roll over.

Families stake their claims
scour the bedrock
to pick out fault cracks
for gold
naked in the heat.

Tent and trailer colonies
gather at bridges
the miners kneel
at the river's banks
swirl sand in pans
appraising gold.

Up higher
the American runs wild
through boulder canyons
white water scours—
crags up Lover's Leap
sever foot trails
in Giant Gap
that pick up
two miles up river
in Green Valley.

The gold gathers
in the bedrock's fissures
and between boulders
in the Gap's
dark, emerald pools—
where there are no trails
in your mettle's ecstasy
light roars
cold—white rush—

Percival Creek

nourished me
    when the salmon spawn
fertilized the filaments
    weaving through its amber.
I looked into my eyes
    and drank.
Fall leaves fell
    from alders and maples
into my rippled reflection.

From that winter
    I plucked a fungus
        and brought it home:
a small fan
    of silver-green filaments
        with ribbon bands
    in burnt-orange and rust.
Worms chewed through its pulp
    escaping in the wind—

Rain fell cold
    and froze on the alder limbs.
I walked back
    through crystal trees
        shattering ice
glistening spray
    fell on leaves
        rotting with salmon.

Five years I returned—
    sunlight flared
        through spring leaves
    into my eyes—
I ran upstream
    through trees
over mossed rocks
    in heat's humid summer.

On the outcropped rock
    between splashing cascades
        and the concrete spillway
balanced
    look into my reflection
where the water's glass
    parts, ripples then shatters
and drink—

Think of salmon:
    flickering, rip-rose flames
splashing up
    glassy spillway steps
or leaping falls—

Sunrise to Arden: American River

Sierra rivers slash
    fissures—carving
        canyon crystal deeper—
sediment collecting cobblestone:
    the Great Valley—
        emerald light
            dancing—swirls
into my eyes
    exploring quiet pool
        grassy—willowy
            ripples that lap
round stone smooth—

Killdeer call
    curls wing's
        wave light—
mist evaporates
    valley oak grove—
        the huge roots suck soil:
nutrients filter up
    thick trunks
        branch
            purple capillaries
leaves breathe—
    moist soft breeze
        my lung tree breathes—

Remember
    the grape vines' juice:
        wild green flames

jungling trees in my youth—
    sun drenched nectar
        quivering illusion
serpent tongues hisssssss—

Years I ran
    from its tendrils
        heat rushing arteries
across raw ribbed cobble tailings
    to the sandstone cliff edge—
        plunge
            deep
        into opaque jade—
the cold grip
    released me
into a dark turbulence:
    adolescent damning
        life blood
flowing to sea.

Wild mallards swoop down
    glide—slide—plash—sheen—
red willow shoots
    off white cobblestone island
bouquet blue heron at point
    poised
        in millennium question.

Clay-sandstone banks erode
    ancient mineral deposits
        feeding live oak grove—
cleared of the jungling
    wild green flames—

roots hang in air
    grasses glistening
        collapse into flow—
I peddle my bicycle by
    on the asphalt trail
        gears tuned
            balance frame
my fashionable figure
    glides in wind—

Jogger, panting, jogs—
    rattlers buzzing—
        a king snake lies broken
            by the wheel—
the cyclist hornet
    radio tuned in virtual reality
        yellow florescent helmet
            screaming logo
"Where is God?"
    passes
        jogger's footsteps plod
easy into   evening   jogs—

Ocean roar in trees—
    box elder's paper pods
        rattling seeds
the waves' spume
    hissssss—

Crows graze
    endlessly feathering
        into
            each other

a field of fruit trees answer
   in chain sawed rows—
the shredder's shriek teeth
   spews evidence:
      suburbia sprawls—

Gulls rise
   from sand bar
      in orchestral swirl—
Mergansers fly low
   over river—whistle wings
      quivering—hovering—pulsing—
streak sunlight brilliance
   illuminating mud, trees, air—
      water rippling gold.

Squirrels scratch
   chase round-up
      cottonwood limb
         whirling
scattering goldfinch
   among alders—

In a handful of elderberries
   tart-sweet juice stains
      my life line river.

Magpies squaaaaaa
   high in eucalyptus
hunters killed
   dime a 'pie—
Now, we preserve

      geese fox   owl   deer   coyote
         coon   beaver   hawk   eagle
            salmon—

Along river shore
    I run over rocks on toes
        hop logs
            duck branch
balance
    stick across—
        breaks—
in mud ooze
    wade through willow shallows.

Salmon fins
    cut green water
        up silver-blue rapid chutes
in clear amber
    silky gravel beds—
silvery-redolent bodies
    thick, heavy
        splashing fins
            squirming riffle redds
squirting eggs with milt
    smooth current.

Crossing over the bridge arc
    I pause, centered—
gulls squawk
    perched on sandstone pedestals
        wait—
crows pick at skeleton salmon

>   stench settles
>   feeding river roots—
> golden crawdads collect
>   for night shift
>   at cobblestones—
> suckers vacuum algae
>   sewage feeds
> their bulging bellies
>   flash bronze
>   feasting
> in late sunlight slant—
>   I cross the bridge:
>   over twenty years
> passing—
>   the evening reflections
>   in electrically lit grids
> aligning the American River.

Salmon State

From university
   I bike east
      on American River bicycle trail—
Leave asphalt
   for dirt road not traveled before
      see what's round
   San Juan Rapids' bend:
two deep, white curls
   we rode in summer.

Ten foot wide dirt road
   dips in a ravine
river on left—pool on right.
   Salmon, centered
      in one inch water
over road—flops heavy—
   stuck—flops
splashing crystal flowers
   rose ripe, fall salmon.

Five to seven pounds
   two feet long
      shining flesh scimitar.
Fish out of water
   I'll eat for a week
      study school tests good
on native brain food!

I stop. Watch it flop.
    Flopping weak
        unable to propel its weight—
My hands
    guide fish's glide—
        tail slap-dives it
into river's opaque jade.

Two fish in pool—
    water level lowers rapidly
for Nimbus Dam Water Diversion Policy.
    One salmon's generations
        equals millions lost.
    Food for thought—
The large salmon
    biggest I've seen
        since fifties
red-black, white
    fungus splotched
        sluggish—
slightly smaller fish
    dark silver-red
        jaws hook!

I splash in—Cold!
    Ten foot wide pool
two feet deep.
    Salmon round-up
splashing silver-rose
    flowers fish frenzy—
corralling biggest fish—
    shove it onto road bed.

The other fish's sense follows
    the grounding—
heave it onto road
    flopping—
shove it into river—safe.

Navigate the slick, ripe
    female, dripping eggs—
easy—forty pounds?
    three feet long
        future's flesh ark
slips from my fingers
    into the American River:
recovering our generation.

Little stream

        sunlight bright

    rapidly flowing

           tumbling delight

Gleaming ray

        precious light

    murmuring stars

         rippling night

Rushing swirling

       morning twilight

    flames licking

        splash light—

Author Biography

Working as a landscaper, laborer, floral farmer and designer, Poet/Teacher Chris Olander has been writing poetry since 1984, "Articulating artistic words through music, spoken word and gestures: poetry experiences of energized body language." Olander's poetry arises from land-based ethics rooted in science, observation and reflection. "I explore human horrors and beautiful auras of mystical revelations and all that is possible in being here now. What we make of life is what we get. I create an action art poetry: musical image phrasing to dramatize relative experiences—a poetry from oral and bard traditions, a sound poet exploring meanings, ideas and emotions in rhythm patterns."

Olander has worked as a Poet/Teacher with California Poets in Schools (CPITS) since 1984. He teaches and reads his work throughout California and in Oregon, Washington and Hawaii. He has been published in many anthologies, magazines and specialty publications. Olander was a founding director of Poet's Playhouse in Nevada City, 1988-99; Nevada County Poetry Series of Grass Valley, 2000-12; an organizer and featured reader for the Berkeley Watershed Environmental Poetry Festival since 2001.

He has read his work accompanied by modern, ballet and Middle Eastern dancers since 1996 at special events and dance recitals and with many musicians using various instruments for 30 years.

www.ingramcontent.com/pod-product-compliance
Lightning Source LLC
Chambersburg PA
CBHW022114090426
42743CB00008B/838